My Mid-Single Mindset

By Doraina Pyle

A special thanks to Al Johnson and Jennie Arrington for their continued support and feedback throughout this endeavor.

To my family, always

1

Introduction

It is our duty to seek to acquire the art of being cheerful since a cheerful spirit will hold in check the demons of despair and stifle the power of discouragement and hopelessness.

- David O. McKay

At the onset of my twenties and a new semester of school, I requested a Priesthood blessing – you know, to receive uplifting counsel from the Lord before the stress began. In all honesty, I was hoping for a bellowing pep talk, something to the effect of, "Good luck – you'll be great! Don't sweat it. Have an awesome year!" Instead, the Lord pronounced, "During your twenties you will be tested and tried even as Abraham was tested and tried."

And well, as always, the Lord was right.

Using brevity, please allow me to summarize: It was hard.

With so many faith-stretching and testimony-building experiences, never was a person more ready and excited to turn thirty than I was. By the time the decade rolled around, I could barely contain my enthusiasm... I jumped out of a plane! I was thrilled to free-fall into the realm of a single adult; more specifically, the world of a mid-single adult.

That's not to say my thirties are without challenges because there are plenty of them. The difference is I understand who I am, what I like and don't like, and what I am capable of achieving. The lessons learned from the previous ten years are now tools at my disposal that help me move forward happily, conquering discouragement and other issues.

Sometimes, however, I feel alone in my positivity and enthusiasm. There is a pervading – even poisoning – Eyore-type mentality among the members of my age-group, evidenced in conversations and observations at activities and online. A particular spirit of "Nobody loves me. Where's my tail?" It is as though my friends feel forgotten by the Lord, left alone to be alone à la Psalm 13. Somehow the Lord seems to remember everyone else on the planet (and beyond) but them, because they reason, if indeed He did remember them, they would be married by now... or at least able to get a date. On the checklist of life, they would have a stellar career, own a house, and have money in the bank.

Nothing could be further from the truth! Neither marital nor worldly status determines whether the Lord remembers us or not. We must rid ourselves of such muddled vision to convert and heal to a correct viewpoint (please ponder Isaiah 6:10/2 Nephi 16:10; Mark 4:12; 3 Nephi 11:5). Then shall we understand Heavenly Father is "mindful of every people" (Alma 26:37) and all His promises will be fulfilled (Isaiah 49:16/1 Nephi 21:16; Alma 50:19; 3 Nephi 1:25 and 27:18). In mercy, "He stretches forth his hands unto [us] all the day long" (Jacob 6:4) for "He loveth our souls" (Alma 24:14). Our Father has tailor-made plans for each of His children; He designed them specifically to help us master weaknesses and realize maximum potential.

As we study the life of Abraham, two points are clear: one, Abraham was promised rich blessings; and two, he encountered numerous trials prior to receiving any of them. Before Abraham was granted the treasures of posterity, Priesthood, and a promised land, he had to endure these tribulations: unnecessary persecution, near-sacrifice and suffering, family death and division, wicked priests, venturing into the great unknown, child-bearing at a laughable age, and willingness to offer his promised and long-awaited offspring to the Lord. (And I would venture this is an abridged list).

Although it was a difficult, less-travelled road, Abraham went forth on it, and on his journey he learned several lessons. Perhaps the most important, Abraham discovered the true nature of Heavenly Father, the power of prayer unto deliverance (Abraham 1:15), and other lessons President Hugh B. Brown has said "Abraham needed to learn about Abraham" (Truman G.

Madsen, The Highest in Us. Salt Lake City: Bookcraft, 1978, 49). Ultimately, Abraham understood the tremendous love his Father in Heaven had for him, and he trusted all promises would be fulfilled.

After great perseverance, the blessings did come – and in abundance. The Lord remembered Abraham, just as he remembered Noah (Genesis 8:1), Rachel (Genesis 30:22), Hannah (1 Samuel 1:19), and his disciples (3 Nephi 28:3 and 4 Nephi 1:14). Likewise, the Lord will remember us, "every creature of his creating" (Mosiah 27:30), and He will grant every blessing promised to us. This means we can take comfort, finding happiness and even joy in the now, before the Lord bestows His other kindnesses.

Naturally, we will need to fight for these blessings. The adversary is well aware of our desires and fights against the fulfillment of them. For example, he thwarts Heavenly Father's plan of eternal families by stopping them before they start. If Satan can make us lose heart, to the point we cease to be social or give up on dating, he has achieved victory. He has waged an aggressive war against our spirits, with a hope we will come to believe "such dreadful things" about Heavenly Father and turn away (*A Grief Observed*, C. S. Lewis, Faber and Faber, 1961).

It is imperative we prepare ourselves as did Abraham to ensure our hearts stay strong. This requires we tweak our acumen of Father's character, believe in our relationship with Him, and increase the profundity of our prayers. As we start this process, the initial hope for fortification will transform into a conviction that produces a faith and development of "real religion that drives out the darkness, rather than simply pacifying us in the midst of darkness" (*Wherefore ye must press forward*, Neal A. Maxwell, Deseret Book Company, 1978). The end results: sure knowledge our Heavenly Father is aware and has a plan for each of us. And of course, a definitive understanding that while life is never going to be perfect, our lives are perfect for us – and for that, we can be happy.

Resourceful gems:

Do Not Despair, Ezra Taft Benson, October 1974 General Conference.
> President Benson offers his 12-step program on how to overcome discouragement and conquer Satan.

Cast Not Away Therefore Your Confidence, Jeffrey R. Holland, March 1999 BYU Devotional.
> Elder Holland instructs to maintain faith in sacred promptings, which often precede wonderful life events.

As a Man Thinketh, James Allen, Bookcraft, 1902.
> A short, but excellent read on how thoughts determine our outlook and actions.

2

The Nature of Our Heavenly Father & Our Relationship to Him

The same Everlasting Father who cares for you today will care for you tomorrow and everyday. Either He will shield you from suffering or give you unfailing strength to bear it. Be at peace then and put aside all anxious thoughts and imaginings.

- St. Frances de Sales

To our Heavenly Father, who loves us all, everybody is a somebody.

- Marvin J. Ashton

A reporter once asked a man, "What do you think of the ignorance and ambivalence of people in the world today?"

The man responded, "I don't know, and I don't care."

(Ah, puns – they make me smile every time!)

In all seriousness, though, sometimes when plans A – Q fail to come together how we hoped they would, we can be tempted to believe our Father in Heaven is much like the man above – that He possesses the same sort of lackadaisical attitude in regards to our life because nothing changes. In grumpiness and near-resentment, we may conclude our contributions were insufficient (and therefore, unaccepted), and there is no justice. And well, thereafter follows a catastrophic tumble, which includes identity loss and submission to the enticements of Lucifer to fill the associated emptiness. To prevent this from happening, we would do well to review the basic principles of the Gospel of Jesus Christ.

In Primary and the mission field, our first lesson is "God is our Heavenly Father. We are His children. He loves us." (The First Presidency, *Preach My Gospel*, Salt Lake City, Bookcraft, 31). These are essential truths, and together, the foundation upon which we base all other doctrines. Because of their importance, the scriptures reiterate these verities. Take, for instance, the creation of the world. As we ponder the accounts of how it happened, we cannot help but notice the deliberation and attention to detail. From the rivers to the mountains, insects to humanity, there is uniqueness, variety, and complexity, not to mention beauty. All testify of the compassion of Heavenly Father. (Is there any wonder, then, why many receive inspiration on mountaintops, in wooded areas, or by the ocean?)

Additionally, the scriptures provide narratives from our predecessors that affirm Heavenly Father has "engraven us upon the palms of his hands; our walls are continually before him" (Isaiah 49:16/1 Nephi 21:16). He helped them cross seas, combat foes, and survive even the most distressing of circumstances. Despite the batter and bruising from hailstorms and fiery darts, they pressed onward. Though at times it was hard, these men and women understood the breadth and depth of the Lord's love through their trials. And like Abraham, they trusted Him and discerned how they were remembered.

But the ultimate manifestation of our Father's care is, of course, the Atonement of Jesus Christ. For in the Garden of Gethsemane, our Savior made payment name-by-name for the mortal mishaps of all who have, are, and will be on this earth.

Without His gift, we would have been forever left in misery with Satan (2 Nephi 9). Thankfully, such is not the case; we can repent. Per John W. Welch: "As we put more effort into learning and understanding God's word, we will also come to a greater understanding of the Atonement of Jesus Christ. The basic meaning of the word atonement is to reconcile two alienated parties."

Now, if our Father is the same yesterday, today, and forever, can we not conclude He possesses equal concern for His children today? With such noted consistency, indeed we *can* reason He is interested and involved. Again, He loves us. Moreover, He is still a God of miracles and has foreordained all of us to succeed.

Said William Law, "If it is said the very hairs of your head are all numbered, is it not to teach us that nothing, not the smallest things imaginable, happen to us by chance? But if the smallest things we can conceive are declared to be under the divine direction, need we, or can we, be more plainly taught that the greatest things of life, such as the manner of our coming into the world, our parents, the time, and other circumstances of our birth and condition, are all according to the eternal purposes, direction, and appointment of Divine Providence?" (*A Serious Call to Devout and Holy Life*, 1729). It is like Mordecai proposed to his cousin Esther: "Who knoweth whether thou art come to the kingdom for such a time as this?" (Esther 4:14).

As we make daily efforts to understand the true nature of God through meticulous scripture study, we will master an accurate perception of our Heavenly Father. He cares, even on our crummiest days, and He remembers us. Though our self-plotted paths may foil, we have still the promised blessings of support, glory, and consolation (Alma 36:27; Doctrine and Covenants 58:3; 2 Corinthians 1:7). As we align our will with Heaven, pulling down our pride in the process, our confidence and love for Heavenly Father and His timing will blossom, and like those who have gone before, we will be able to move forward in peace.

Resourceful gems:

In the Strength of the Lord, David A. Bednar, October 2001
BYU Devotional.
> Elder Bednar discusses the enabling power of the
> Atonement, which changes our fallen natures from bad to
> good to better.

The Mediator, Boyd K. Packer, April 1977 General Conference.
> Elder Packer delivers one of the best explanations of the
> Atonement by way of parable.

Our Last Chance, Sheri L. Dew, April 1999 General Conference.
> Sister Dew relates how a personal incident which left her
> stranded helped her better understand the love expressed in
> the Atonement.

The Purifying Power of Gethsemane, Bruce R. McConkie, April
1985 General Conference.
> This is Elder McConkie's incredibly moving testimony of
> Jesus Christ.

3

Meaningful Prayer

Life is fragile, and therefore, should be handled with prayer.

- Harold B Lee

The most important of your planning should be on your knees.

- Ezra Taft Benson

By this point in our lives, I think we can safely conclude *life is unpredictable*. Let's face it – things happen. And not that I speak from personal experience or anything, but... sometimes your keys fall into the toilet or your hair gets stuck on the fence as the crowd presses forward. Life is a crazy mélange of humor and frustration, joy and sorrow, and beauty and pain, where even the best laid plans can go awry. With all its variables, it seems the only way to survive while maintaining a positive outlook is with meaningful prayer.

Throughout the scriptures, we find multiple instances where we have been instructed to petition the Lord, as well as examples of prayer and the blessings that follow from offering our hearts to Father. Among these, we have Amulek, who counseled we pray everywhere and for everything, including crops, flocks, resistance to the devil, and prosperity (see Alma 34:17-27). Then there was Matthew, who suggested shutting our doors to pray in secret (Matthew 6:6); Hannah, who epitomized sincerity (1 Samuel 1 & 2); and Daniel, who manifested humility and amazing faith (Daniel 9).

But the two prayers of upmost importance are those from which spring the greatest events of this earth's history: namely, the Atonement of Jesus Christ and the Restoration of his Gospel to the earth today (please see and study John 17 and Joseph Smith History). As a result of these heartfelt supplications, the entire human race receives salvation and full knowledge of the Gospel of Jesus Christ. How incredible is that? Not to mention, joyful!

As we study the particulars of these experiences, we notice similarities. No doubt Joseph mirrored the example of the Savior, for in both we find the following traits:

- Each sought solitude in a quiet place.

- Both knelt and prayed vocally, with real intent.

- The two expressed what was in their hearts, believing Heavenly Father was there and would answer.

- When temptation surfaced, each overcame, and miracles resulted.

Now, if we wish to survive the loneliness and other difficulties Satan fires continuously at Mid-Singles, should not we do likewise? That is, offer our hearts to Father privately with sincerity and purpose, believing miracles will occur? Should not we strive to have meaningful prayer each time we kneel? If your desire is bona fide, please do pray "the food strengthen and nourish your body," "the missionaries be led to the pure in heart," and "to travel in safety so no harm or accident will befall you" – just remember to slow down as you make these requests. If, however, your prayers have become rote, akin to the popular introductory testimony expression "for those of you who don't know me, my name is _____," chances are meaning has been lost. As seminary teachers worldwide emphasize, "Sure we think to pray, but when we pray, do we think?"

From A. Theodore Tuttle: "It should have great meaning that of all the titles of respect and honor and admiration that could be given Him, that God Himself, He who is the highest of all, chose to be addressed simply as Father" (*The Role of Fathers*, Ensign, January 1974, 66). There is an unmistakable connection to Deity once we recognize our family tie, and there will be a remarkable difference in how we offer our prayers as we understand the significance of our Divine lineage.

In the jungle of life, it might be best to adopt specific times to render proper prayer, so we can have more than trite "How are you? Fine" conversations. If morning is not your friend, then set aside a moment when you are awake. If you are secretly an eighty-year-old trapped in thirty-year-old body, offer your heartfelt words before fatigue sets in at night. If your sole alone time exists on your commute, then turn your car into a "secret place" where you can express raw feelings and listen for responses. When and where possible, find opportunities to pray – volunteer, so leaders, teachers, and officiators do not have to beg.

The blessings that stem from prayer are multifold. Not only can we stay close to the Spirit and receive revelation, as we entreat the Lord we can maintain faith in promptings – even the ones that seem ridiculously-crazy, like sacrificing a child (see Genesis 22) – and find needed answers. We can welcome inspiration for callings and other service, remain protected, help loved ones, and find our way home without panicking. Prayer helps us cultivate gratitude and develop other Christlike attributes; it provides the ability to practice self-discipline and forgive others. And at this time in our life where we may have questions, prayer grants us the ability to trust the Lord and His timing, feel His love and maintain hope, as well as appreciate our more humorous moments.

As we follow the pattern of meaningful prayer Jesus Christ set forth, we will be blessed with miracles specific to our needs. Prayer will forge our connection with Heavenly Father and provide a sure knowledge of His love and plan for each of us. Surely then will we survive our Mid-Singleton years with grace and poise – and maybe even a few laughs.

Resourceful gems:

The Lord's Prayer Skit
Given to me as a teenager by one of my young women leaders, this has forever impacted my viewpoint on what constitutes meaningful prayer. A man begins to pray, but then God interrupts...
http://witnessdragon.tripod.com/lordprayerskit.htm

Prayer, Ezra Taft Benson, April 1977 General Conference.
President Benson shares key ways to have meaningful prayer. Notice the poem he learned as a youth – it encapsulates the beauty and trust rendered in prayer.

To Draw Closer to God, Henry B. Eyring, April 1991 General Conference.
President Eyring explains how coming closer to Heavenly Father is similar to the steps we take to stay near to a dear friend.

Trust in the Lord, Richard G. Scott, October 1995 General Conference.
This is the touching and faith-filled testimony of Elder Scott about placing our faith in our Father and His wisdom through prayer.

4

Repentance

With thoughtless and impatient hands

We tangle up the plans

The Lord hath wrought.

And when we cry in pain, He saith,

"Be quiet, man, while I untie the knot."

- Anonymous

Once upon a summer, I participated in a play with a guy named Vincent. He was sweet and incredibly fun, but every day for six weeks Vincent would talk about his need to lose weight when he would come to rehearsal. Apparently, he found his size problematic. So, when performance time arrived, en lieu of the standard "good show" candy, I bought Vincent a set of nice pencils. On the card, I wrote, "Vincent, I would've given you chocolate, but you said you were going on a diet." Given his daily concern, I felt this best, and of course, most thoughtful on my part.

Approximately seven weeks later, I saw Vincent at school, and to my surprise discovered he had lost a tremendous amount of weight. When I caught up to him, he revealed the total was *40 to 45 pounds*.

"Vincent, that's incredible," I said to him. "Congratulations! I am so proud of you."

Then he looked at me… and the question formed on his lips: "Doraina, you know what finally pushed me to go on a diet, don't you?"

"No, I don't," I answered truthfully.

"It was you."

"Me? What? I'm confused."

"Doraina, do you remember the good show gift you gave me?"

"Yes, I gave you pencils."

"And do you remember what you wrote on the card?"

"Yes. I wrote, 'Vincent, I would have given you chocolate, but you said you were going on a diet."

With sad eyes and a grave voice, he said, "No, Doraina, that's not what you wrote. You wrote, 'Vincent, I would've given you chocolate, but you *should* go on a diet.'"

Yeah.

It was pretty bad.

Imagine my horror.

As humans, it's inevitable: we make mistakes. Try as we may to live up to the command to be perfect, there are moments (of varying degree and frequency) we mess up. For most, we understand all-too-well the concept "all have sinned and fall short of the glory of God" (Romans 3:23). In Sunday school, however, we have learned there is hope! Through and because of Jesus Christ, we have repentance, which allows us to change from sinful to clean behavior. Our Brother's Atonement enables us to surmount spiritual death, or the division that separates us from Father when we sin; it satisfies the demands of justice which otherwise require full accountability for our actions. We have been taught that as we activate the power that comes through this great Act of Mercy in our lives, we can be healed, and the pressures that weigh down our hearts will be relieved.

Yet despite this knowledge, as Mid-singletons we sometimes feel our aberrant behavior has marked us for infinite solitude. From here through eternity, we are destined to be alone. In some cases, we think we botched matters so tremendously we now suffer God's punishment. Else why would we not be granted the greatest desires of our hearts? Why aren't we married? Why don't we have children? We have kept the commandments and given our all, but the Lord has not provided, so surely something is wrong because we have no explanation. In our abject state, we proclaim, "I am forgotten." We compare, "Everything came together for her," and we judge, "He doesn't deserve it." In fear, some of us even exclaim, "Ergh, the time clock is ticking!"

It is amazing how closely we listen to and believe the whisperings of Satan. The truth is even if we were the most righteous, we could still be single – it all depends on the Lord's plan for the individual. And we each have a plan! Thus we can take comfort we are not stamped for endless solitude because of a misstep. In fact, Heavenly Father has promised the riches of eternity (please see Doctrine and Covenants 78:17-22). We must learn to trust Him, to understand His loving nature, and to believe the Gospel of Jesus Christ. Our value is not based on where we are in life relative to another person.

Back to the introductory story: when my error was unveiled, my chin hit the floor. Then, with full understanding of the impact of such an egregious mistake, my body proceeded into shut-down mode. Vincent grabbed and shook my shoulders to prevent me from going into a literal state of shock. At last, recovering in small part, I found myself repeating with a feeble voice, "Vincent, I am so sorry." My friend squared me to face him and meeting my eyes, he said, "Doraina, I forgive you."

As we forsake sin and spurn our favorite vices, so, too, does Heavenly Father state we are forgiven and He will remember our sins no more (Doctrine and Covenants 58:42). He loves us. Our Father desires to bless us, which is why He commands we be worthy of the blessings we seek. He wants us to return to live with Him someday and has provided a means whereby we can through His Son Jesus Christ. Let us renew our hope and testimony of Father and the individual plan He has tailored for each of us, seeking always to do our best and to repent as needed.

Resourceful gem

The Miracle of Forgiveness, Spencer W. Kimball, Bookcraft, 1969, particularly chapters 22 and 23.

>Despite the diverse and numerous ways we can sin, President Kimball testifies our Father has provided a successful means whereby we can repent and be forgiven through His Son, Jesus Christ.

5

Loving Our Neighbor

We must develop the capacity to see men not as they are at present but as they may become. We need to be told that we amount to something, that we are capable and worthwhile.

Thomas S. Monson

Sometimes Jesus' command to "Love one another" (John 13:34) feels like an improbable, if not impossible, task. As soon as our feet hit the floor, it is as though we must deal with a continual stream of interactions: running into the neighbor, getting caught in traffic, ascending the elevator with the guy from seventh, handling clients and co-workers, checking our email, and waiting in line (to name a few). Truth be told, some of these exchanges go better than others. I imagine if we could stay in bed all day, it would be easy to maintain charity. The Lord, however, requires us to move, and consequently, there are good, bad, and less-than-pretty interchanges with others.

After all –

imperfect human + imperfect human = imperfect interaction

In order to change the equation to increase the likelihood of an amiable relationship, we must insert Perfection. To do this requires 1), strengthening our connection with Heavenly Father, and 2), utilizing the enabling power of the Atonement of Jesus Christ. As we implore heaven's aid, we develop *heavenly* attributes, including love (which is at the heart of our two steps). We gain the capacity to look past selfishness and weaknesses, such as "me³" mentalities, instant gratification, and irresponsibility. We are blessed with the ability to see our fellowman as our brothers and sisters – children of God with divine potential and purpose.

This means we share Father's vision of seeing others for what they can become, not as who they are now. Never would we perceive Saul as "the least of all the families of the tribe of Benjamin" (1 Samuel 9:21) or classify Moses as ineloquent (Exodus 4:10). Enoch would not be slow of speech, hated by others (Moses 6:31), nor would Joseph be as "an obscure boy… doomed to the necessity of obtaining a scanty maintenance by his daily labor" (Joseph Smith History 1:23). From humble beginnings, these men became prophets. Our Savior was more than a carpenter; He is the Son of God (see Mark 6:1-5).

The point is, despite human frailties our actual and online entourage can butterfly into persons amazing, especially with love and the Gospel of Jesus Christ. Think of Zeezrom from the Book of Mormon. When first introduced, he is a stealthy lawyer without convictions, who perpetuates contention for monetary gain. Because of his actions, Alma and Amulek were unduly imprisoned and forced to watch a martyrdom of believers (Alma chapters 11-15). After his conversion, though, he became a missionary that accompanied Alma to teach the Zoramites (Alma 31:6, 32; Helaman 5:41), and later a city was named in his honor (Alma 56:14). In his journal, I am sure there are miracles similar to Alma, Amulek, and the sons of Mosiah.

Now, please don't misunderstand. Some situations require more than Christlike love; they need counsel and action. When face-to-face with the negative (in person or online), let the Spirit be your guide with focus and approach. Go to the temple. Surely, there are "good, better, and best" ways to express ourselves while upholding the Savior's command to be charitable (*Good, Better, Best*, Dallin H. Oaks, October 2007 General Conference). We should be "bold, but not overbearing" (Alma 38:12), "showing forth afterwards an increase of love" (Doctrine and Covenants 121:43).

Said Sister Sheri Dew, "What we have in common... is so much more significant than any distinctions in our individual lives" (*No Doubt About It*, Deseret Book, 2002, p. 225). As we strengthen our bond with Heavenly Father and draw from the Savior's Sacrifice, we will be able to find and focus on these commonalities. With unity, our relationships will improve, as will our level of contentment. Then shall we "love one another" and recognize divine potential without reservations.

Resourceful Gems:

The Tongue Can Be A Sharp Sword, Marvin J. Ashton, April 1992 General Conference.

> Elder Ashton goes into the importance of being (and becoming) charitable toward others (to include giving the benefit of the doubt and refraining from bashing, which is ever-so-needed today – especially online).

See Others as They May Become, Thomas S. Monson, October 2012 General Conference.

> President Monson confirms men and women can change for the better when we focus on their divine potential, rather than their mortal frailties.

6

Service

My life is like my shoes, to be worn out in service.

- Spencer W Kimball

On our way home one afternoon, my mom stopped to give food to a homeless woman standing on the street corner. (My mom always keeps packaged items in the car for distribution; she figures it is the least she can do). As she placed the Poptarts in outstretched hands, the woman smiled at my mother in recognition, her front teeth missing, and said: "I was hoping you would come. I've been so hungry."

My mother, AKA "the Poptart lady" to some around town, is the heroine of my life. When I was a child, she tended to elderly women needing assistance. On holidays, she would cook pies and serve food at different shelters. Every Sunday she picks up the chapel so other wards sharing the building can have a meaningful Sacrament experience sans paper and food distractions. She cares for my uncle, who is almost completely disabled, and until recently, she looked after my grandma, a woman who was well advanced in Alzheimer's. My mom would feed her, wash her feet, and do her laundry. It can be said that no matter what service is needed, my mother will help, and she will do so without complaint. Again, according to her, it's the least she can do.

Obviously, my mother patterns her life after the Savior. When Jesus Christ was on the earth, He visited the widow and the orphan alike, fed the hungry, and cared for the poor. He made time for that which was important – that is, His brothers and sisters. With love as his motivation, Jesus offered Himself as an eternal sacrifice, suffering on our behalf in the Garden of Gethsemane and on the cross. Because of his choice, we have the glorious opportunity to spend a joyous eternity with Him and Heavenly Father. Today, through the Spirit, the resurrected Christ strengthens us as we struggle and offers comfort when we are brokenhearted

With Jesus as our example, the standard for service is set, and it is one that requires kindness, or an ability to look beyond oneself toward others. How else can we "lift up the hands which hang down, and strengthen the feeble knees" (Doctrine and Covenants 81:5)?

At times, however, providing service may seem difficult, especially for Mid-Singles. There is a constant battle for our time and priorities. And with our natural selves, we are prone to rationalize "I'm too busy" or "That doesn't concern me." Basically, we would rather do what we want to do, albeit posting "selfies" or playing video games. We've got to exercise, we need to sleep, or we must spend time with our significant other, who we left moments ago. Fill in the blank as appropriate. There are all kinds of excuses, which frankly, are egocentric at best. Remember, "Christ never brushed aside those in need because He had bigger things to do!" (*Put Off the Natural Man, and Come Off Conqueror*, Neal A. Maxwell, October 1990 General Conference).

Said Brigham Young, "Let every individual in this city feel the same interest for the public good as he does for his own, and you will at once see this community still more prosperous and still more rapidly increasing in wealth, influence, and power, but where each one seeks to benefit himself or herself alone, and does not cherish a feeling for prosperity and benefit of the whole, that people will be disorderly, unhappy, and poverty stricken, and distress, animosity, and strife will reign" (*Journal of Discourses*, 1856, p. 330).

Now you may be thinking, "Yeah, yeah, I've heard that before. I understand this is important, but really I do have a busy schedule. How can I actuate service into my life?" Or perhaps you feel inadequate and wonder "What can I do?" These are both excellent questions. To answer, we need only to examine service itself. To serve is to render aid or help to another – period. Please notice there are no conditions of size, time, or manner of service. Although we understand this on a certain level, too often in application we view service as an organized, calendared program – grandiose in composition and taxing of our time, like an all-day charity event. Hence the reason we feel unable or incapable of incorporation; we forget small acts of kindness are veritable deeds of service, but even the ant can help the peony to bloom.

My advice, therefore, to Martha and Enoch alike, is to start with inspiration you receive to do good, and then *act* on it! Whether you feel impressed to make a long-overdue phone call or to mow your neighbor's lawn, if the action leads you to bless the life of another, it is service, and it is heaven-sent. President Monson has counseled "Never, never, never postpone following a prompting" (*The Spirit Giveth Life*, April 1985 General Conference), and Sister Parkin has advised, "Never suppress a generous thought" (*Personal Ministry: Sacred and Precious*, February 2007 BYU Devotional). These strokes of inspiration are occasions to minister as did the Savior. As you hearken to the promptings you receive, your service will answer another child's prayer. The more you heed these calls, the more opportunities will be given to you. And as you act, you will find greater happiness.

For those who struggle with ideas of how to serve, please find below my list of simple actions that make a positive difference in the lives of others and in my level of contentment:

1) Perform one act of service for a family member daily.

2) Reach out to at least one individual a day (preferably in person or by phone).

3) Be a 100 percent home or visiting teacher, and allow yourself to be home or visit taught each month. Change "If there is anything I can do for you, let me know" to "What can I do for you?"

4) Attend the temple regularly, and if possible, become a temple worker.

5) Find a community service opportunity and commit to it. There are numerous options available at justserve.org and elsewhere online.

As we extend beyond ourselves, finding the least *we* can do to serve our brothers and sisters, our level of happiness will increase, and our obsession with "single-dom" and other problems will dissipate. The Lord provides countless opportunities for us to reach outward and uplift one another; we need but listen and act on His inspiration. And as an added bonus, our Father has promised to honor every service rendered with an equal return of such kindness (see Alma 41:14-15).

Resourceful gems:

Personal Ministry: Sacred and Precious, Bonnie D. Parkin, February 2007 BYU Devotional.
>   Present when this message on our definite and distinct ministry was delivered, this discourse changed my life and attitude while in graduate school.

A Poor Wayfaring Man of Grief, James Montgomery, 1826, all seven stanzas. Known as Hymn 29 in LDS Hymnbooks.
>   The perfect illustration of how when we are in the service of our fellow beings we are only in the service of our God (Mosiah 2:17). No wonder the Prophet Joseph loved it!

7

Dating

Don't complain. Just do it. You can't go through life sucking on

a pickle. "

- Gordon B. Hinckley

Let's be honest – dating is like driving: we all think we are good at it, and the other person is always at fault. And so, in frustration we condemn the red light runner and the guy who didn't signal, and strain our necks to check out the catastrophe nearby. A bit disgruntled, we may utilize particular gestures or unkind words, which we know are unbecoming of a disciple of Jesus Christ. On the roads and in dating, we must dig deep to muster patience as we motor toward our destination.

The truth is in the quest to love and be loved everyone can improve in one way or another. While we could place blame on varying daters (as we do drivers), we would do well to first conduct a self-check – to ensure we are at operating at optimum level. As we do so, we may find it is we who need to change speed or our routines, eliminate distractions, or even signal more clearly. I propose, therefore, we regularly service and do the following on our mechanical checklist:

☐	Be happy!
	Few will dispute that happy people radiate! Because they find peace and joy in the everyday, happy people exhibit confidence about life and themselves. They smile, proving true the adage, "A merry heart maketh a cheerful countenance" (Proverbs 15:3). They are social. For them, the glass has liquid that tastes good and satisfies. Their ability to focus on the positive allows them to forego the desire to nit-pick and surmount the temptation to feel alienated.
	We, too, can have such an outlook, even if life is different than what we had planned. We can bear testimony and express gratitude often, counting our blessings daily. We can serve because, after all, "happiness is really a by-product of service" (*As I Have Loved You*, Robert L. Backman,

October 1985 General Conference). When friends get engaged, we can celebrate; when babies come along, we can rejoice! We can congratulate those who get promoted and be excited at others people's success. The Lord has promised as we rid ourselves of "jealousies and fears, and humble [our]selves before [the Lord]," then "shall [we] see [the Lord] and know that [He is]" (Doctrine and Covenants 67:10)

☐ Get our ducks in a row.

There is no time like the present to begin a career, pay off debts, organize food storage, get healthy, learn domestic skills, work on genealogy, continue education, open an IRA, complete projects, get involved in the community, magnify callings, develop talents, overcome addictions, unplug, and learn how to best manage our time. As we do so, not only will we find a sense of self (and therefore, increased cheer), we will be able to contribute positively to the world around us and to a relationship when it comes along.

	(For other suggestions, please read *Becoming a Somebody* by John H. Vandenberg, October 1972 General Conference.)
☐	Learn independence. We were created as individuals, blessed with minds to make decisions and hearts to determine feelings. This means we can function in such a capacity, using the bathroom by ourselves or operating without a wingman. In any relationship, maintain your identity, for co-dependence paralyzes and stifles progression.
☐	Set social goals. Decide the level and degree of your social activity. How often will you get out each month? How many people will you introduce yourself to when there? Will you host activities yourself? Invite ward families over for dinner? Have the missionaries? As with anything, social activity is all what you make of it. The more you put in, the more you get out of it. You increase your chances of finding "the one" when you move

	beyond the front door.
	Start small and work your way up. Begin by calling someone you haven't talked to in a while or messaging someone online. Send an email. Practice the art of small-talk as introduce yourself to someone at church or at an activity.
☐	Be honest with feelings.
	An inch of honesty is worth a pound of cure (from embarrassment and heartache, to say the least).
	While the world would have us think dating is some sort of game, with gospel perspective, we know it is much more than that. It is a pre-cursor to eternal courtship, AKA marriage, which is part of our Father's great plan of happiness. It is okay, therefore, to say, "Hey, I would like to get to know you better" or "No, I'm not interested, but can we be friends?" And, at times, "You seem like such a nice person. Do you have a child my age I could date?"
	Obviously, employ kindness. Love is communication at its

	best. The Lord would never want us to have "a mind to injure one another, but to live peaceably" (Mosiah 4:13).
☐	Get comfortable with commitment. No more of this maybe I'll come… unless something better comes along. When invited to an activity, provide a yes or no. If you say you will be there, then be there. If you promise someone you will call or write, do so. Channel the boy scout within (Trustworthy, loyal, helpful, friendly…).
☐	Stay clean. Yes, yes, we all have needs, but our Father has given specific dos and don'ts about moral purity that cannot be rationalized. He has commanded repeatedly for us to keep His commandments, which include maintaining our standards of virtue and integrity. If you drift, repent. The Lord loves the Prodigals.

Now that we have 'auto-tuned,' let us shift gears to the important topic of communication. (By way of example…) At the commencement of graduate school, the Bishopric of my ward distributed a dating questionnaire for all members of the congregation to complete. We were encouraged to be truthful in our responses, and full anonymity was promised. When the questionnaires were returned, copies were made for leadership to review. Upon careful study, leadership found the answers revealed an interesting polarity between the male and female mindsets.

In response to the question "What are your frustrations about dating?" most, if not all, of the men gave this response: "I hate the pressure associated with dating, and I hate having to come up with something creative. I don't like being told I'm not living up to my Priesthood if I'm not dating. And no, I can't just ask a girl out because if I do, she's going to think I want to marry her and will start planning our wedding."

The girls, in turn, wrote answers to this effect: "I want a chance! You don't have to plan anything creative; you don't need to do something elaborative. Come over to my apartment, have some hot chocolate, and talk to me. I'm not going to start planning our wedding – trust me. I have to get to know you before I fall in love with you. Again, I just want a chance!"

Did you catch the irony? Astounding, if not incredulous, isn't it? Here we live in a world where we have an abundance of interactive technology, to include phones, texts, emails, and social media. And yet, we cannot seem to communicate important basic messages across gender lines. I mean in theory, with today's technology, one could have a fatal accident, resulting in fractured vertebrae, pulmonary contusions, and a concussion, and could *still* find a way to convey a message to another person. (Well, maybe once he had recovered).

With this situation, once the Bishopric and other ward leaders pinpointed the problem – namely, communication or the lack thereof – they cleared the air by cross-sharing sentiments in Elders Quorum and Relief Society. Miraculously, post-discussion, people started dating... getting engaged...and married. By the end of the year, our ward had almost four times the number of marriages in the stake and area than the ward with the second highest number (fifteen compared to four).

If we were to look to and follow the Lord's method of communication, we would utilize plainness and simplicity. Our Father desires we learn and understand, hence the reason He is clear and forthright (2 Nephi 3:12; 25:4; 31:3). With full knowledge, there is progression and unity. Then, not only does the quality of our relationships improves, miracles happen. Look at the people in the City of Zion, who did "flourish" with the blessings of the Lord because they were of "one heart and of one mind," dwelling in righteousness (Moses 7:17-18). Or, take those from 4 Nephi, who dealt "justly one with another" and "were married, and given in marriage, and were blessed according to the multitude of the promises which the Lord had made unto them" (verses 2 and 11).

As my mom says, dating is supposed to be a pleasant experience. May it be so for all of us as we strive to improve ourselves and our communication across gender lines. Then shall we make it to our destinations in peace – and with fewer injuries.

Resourceful gems:

For All Eternity; A Four-Talk Set on How to Strengthen Your Marriage CD set, Dr. John L. Lund, Covenant Communications, Inc., 2003.
> Through humor and with multiple examples, Dr. Lund stresses the importance of real communication between men and women (not just hinting).

Dating versus Hanging Out, Dallin H. Oaks, June 2006 Ensign (originally delivered in May 2005 at a CES fireside).
> Straightforward as always, Elder Oaks defines dating and proper courtship in an effort to eradicate issues and problems some may be experiencing.

To the Single Adult Brethren of the Church AND *To the Single Adult Sisters of the Church*, President Ezra Taft Benson, April and October 1988 respectively, General Conference.
> Separate counsel to the singles of the church from a prophet of the Lord. And while the address to the sisters was read by President Monson, it was delivered with the same love and meaning that was given to the brethren (and as President Benson intended).

8

Conclusion

To every thing there is a season . . .

- Ecclesiastes 3

A time to hear the thunder and a time to ponder silence,

A time to see the storm and a time to witness the beauty of the

rainbow.

-Paul H. Dunn

My brothers and sisters, if there is anything we learn from the life of Abraham, it is that although life is hard, we can move forward in faith and happiness. In due time, all blessings promised will be granted. Our Father has a wonderful plan for each of His children, which includes fulfilling the innermost desires of our hearts. He has not forgotten you. He loves you. Heavenly Father knows your dreams, and He hears your pleadings. Stay strong in the Gospel; fight for your blessings. As we do our part to increase our understanding of His true nature, improve our prayers, and serve one another, then shall each of us be blessed with a sunnier mid-single mindset.

About the Author

Photo courtesy of Bonnie Hill of Goodenough Photography

Doraina Pyle is an author, speaker, and personal development coach who desires to "Make a positive difference." Much of her time is spent as a volunteer at church and in the community. In 2003, she earned a Dual Bachelor's degree in French Studies and English Composition from the University of North Texas. In 2009, she completed a Masters in Language Acquisition and Teaching at Brigham Young University. In her spare time, Doraina enjoys reading, dancing, piano, and travel. She is an avid seeker of self-improvement and finds joy in the beauty of living simply.

For more information, please visit www.DorainaPyle.com.

www.ingramcontent.com/pod-product-compliance
Lightning Source LLC
Chambersburg PA
CBHW071736020426
42331CB00008B/2057